M000023939

VIRGINIA
Simply Beautiful II

PHOTOGRAPHY BY **CHARLES GURCHE**

FARCOUNTRY PRESS

RIGHT: Puckett Cabin on the Blue Ridge Parkway was the last home of Orlean Hawks Puckett, a midwife who assisted in the births of more than one thousand Virginians from 1890 to 1939.

TITLE PAGE: At Arlington National Cemetery, this monument marks the grave of General George Crook (1828-1890), one of the U.S. Army's most skilled Indian fighters but also an advocàte for Indians' rights. The Sioux chief Red Cloud praised Crook for dealing honestly with his people.

FRONT COVER: The historic Sinking Creek Bridge, near Pearlsburg in Giles County, is a seventy-foot span that dates from 1916.

BACK COVER: Jones Run Falls plunges through the forest in Shenandoah National Park.

ISBN 10: 1-56037-401-2
ISBN 13: 978-1-56037-401-5
Photography © 2006 by Charles Gurche
© 2006 Farcountry Press

For more information about our books write Farcountry Press, P.O. Box 5630, Helena, MT 59604; call (800) 821-3874; or visit www.farcountrypress.com.

Created, produced, and designed in the United States.
Printed in China.

10   09   08   07   06   1   2   3   4   5

Introduction

by Charles Gurche

One spring, I woke well before sunrise in the Big Meadows Campground in Shenandoah National Park. Although it was late May, the dawn was chilly after a clear night. As I drove to Skyline Drive, I passed deer nibbling on the spring grass. Oaks, just beginning to leaf out, were silhouetted against the glowing eastern sky. The road wove along the spine of the Blue Ridge, passing overlooks and cliff tops.

At the Hazel Mountain Overlook, an expansive view of the hollows, surrounding mountains, and valleys below opened up before me. Pockets of fog had settled into low-lying areas overnight. The potential for strong photographs looked promising, and I set up and focused the 4x5 camera. The sun rose, illuminating the fog, fields, and hills with golden light. I quickly exposed a few sheets of film of simple compositions. I imagined similar scenes occurring across Virginia that morning, each embellished with morning light and patchy fog.

Follow the outline of Virginia and the state's great diversity becomes apparent. Starting at Virginia's northernmost point, the border wiggles its way southwest for about 500 miles, following high mountain ridges and crossing deep gorges such as Breaks Interstate State Park and the New River Valley. Search these rugged mountains of western Virginia and you'll discover many incredible places such as Cascade Falls, Mountain Lake, Dragon's Tooth, and Falling Spring.

From Cumberland Gap, where the tip of Virginia meets Kentucky and Tennessee, the border turns east, crossing more steep country and clear streams. At the mountain town of Damascus, hikers head out on the Appalachian Trail and bicyclists ride the Virginia Creeper Trail with its forty-seven trestles. Further east, the line crosses the Blue Ridge Parkway. Beginning in 1935, this 469-mile national park road was constructed in order to conserve and provide public access to the cultural, historical, and natural resources of the Appalachian Mountains.

The state line then descends to the Piedmont area, passing historic towns such as Halifax and Clarksville, where antebellum homes reflect the early settlement of this region. The Piedmont is bordered by the Blue Ridge Mountains to the west and the Tidewater region to the east. This is the land of Thomas Jefferson, Booker T. Washington, James Madison, and Robert E. Lee. Continuing east, the state line passes swamps such as the Great Dismal Swamp National Wildlife Refuge, which hosts prehistoric-looking stands of water tupelo and bald cypress trees. Further east, it passes saltwater estuaries and Back Bay, then runs

ABOVE: Arlington House, at Arlington National Cemetery, was built from 1802 to 1815 by George Washington Custis, grandson of Martha Washington. When Robert E. Lee married George Custis's daughter Mary, he began thirty years' residence here, which ended when he left to head the Army of the Confederacy.

on to False Cape State Park on the Atlantic.

From here, Virginia's coastal barrier islands and sandy beaches extend north more than 100 miles. Just inland, up the James River, is the site of Jamestown, the nation's oldest permanent settlement, which began in 1607, thirteen years before the pilgrims landed at Plymouth Rock. Nearby, Williamsburg provides a glimpse of the eighteenth century, with more than 100 original and 400 reconstructed buildings. Not far away at Yorktown, General Cornwallis surrendered to George Washington on October 17, 1781–the sixth year of the American Revolution. Further north, Assateague Island National Seashore is continuously being shaped by wind and water. In the 1600s, colonists grazed horses on the island and the descendants of these herds remain today. Nearby, Chincoteague National Wildlife Refuge hosts more than 300 bird species.

Heading west now, the state line crosses forty miles of Chesapeake Bay and then follows the south bank of the Potomac River past George Washington's birthplace, now the George Washington National Monument, and further north, his home at Mount Vernon. Both sites look much as they did in the eighteenth century with period buildings, furniture, and gardens. Farther north toward Washington, D.C., is Alexandria, first settled in the 1670s. Inland, the Manassas National Battlefield Park commemorates the First Battle of Bull Run, the first major battle of the Civil War, where Stonewall Jackson earned his nickname.

The state line follows the Potomac upstream to Great Falls Park, where

CTION·1898–1902 × BOXER·REBELLION·1900 × NICARAGUA·1912 × VERA·CRUZ·1914 × HAITI·1915–1934 × SANTO·DOMINGO·1916–1924 × WORLD·WAR·1·1917–1918 BELLEAU·WOOD·SOISSO
4 × GRENADA · 1983 × PERSIAN·GULF·1987–1991 × PANAMA· 1988–1990 ·

ABOVE: President Dwight Eisenhower dedicated this bronze U.S. Marine Corps Memorial at Arlington National Cemetery in 1954. Sculptor Felix W. de Weldon based it on the 1945 Joe Rosenthal news photograph taken as four marines and a Navy corpsman raised the flag on Iwo Jima in the South Pacific.

expert kayakers boat in the wild waters. Farther northeast, near historic Harpers Ferry, West Virginia, the Potomac receives the waters of the Shenandoah River near our starting point. Virginia's abundant mountains, rivers, forests, shorelines, towns, and historic sites offer a lifetime of discovery.

While photographing Virginia, I searched for ways to convey the essence of each particular place. In my images, I sought strong compositions and striking light or seasonal conditions, hoping to bring the place to life. Backlit greens of early spring, delicate coatings of frost in the forest, the pink and purple pastels of early-morning light: I wanted these special scenes to communicate the harmony, beauty, or soul of a particular place.

I have had the good fortune to photograph Virginia for fifteen years. I am grateful to the dozens of Virginians who helped in all aspects of traveling, from offering advice to helping me locate places to photograph. Their kindness and generosity were essential in the completion of this project and will not be forgotten. I hope these photographs may inspire others to head out and experience the rich cultural, historical, and natural resources of Virginia.

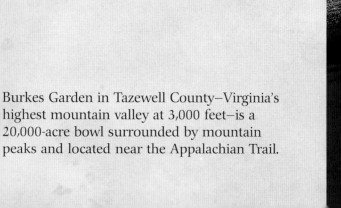

Burkes Garden in Tazewell County—Virginia's highest mountain valley at 3,000 feet—is a 20,000-acre bowl surrounded by mountain peaks and located near the Appalachian Trail.

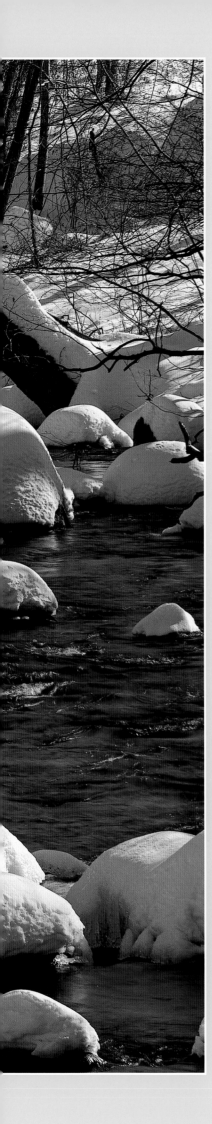

RIGHT: Its lacy leaves gone, a native locust tree sports a froth of white.

LEFT: The Hughes River, one of Shenandoah National Park's fishing streams, meanders among boulders covered in winter's velvet.

BELOW: Straightstone Creek flows toward the Staunton River through central Virginia's Pittsylvania County, which was named for British statesman William Pitt–honoring his opposition to the Stamp Act that infuriated American colonists.

RIGHT: The Hogcamp Branch of the Rose River whispers serenely over moss-covered rocks on a lazy summer day.

FACING PAGE: North Creek cascades over the rocks amid Jefferson National Forest's 703,000 acres in southwestern Virginia, a home to bears, deer, and wild turkeys.

LEFT AND BELOW: Virginia Beach, a popular destination for Virginians and vacationers from throughout the eastern United States, boasts twenty-eight miles of beach and thirty-eight miles of coastline. PHOTOS BY RICHARD NOWITZ

RIGHT: This massive bridge crosses the Rappahannock River at Fredericksburg. In December of 1862, lack of a bridge slowed U.S. Army General Ambrose Burnside's advance toward Fredericksburg, which was finally made on pontoon bridges that were built under Confederate fire.

BELOW: Under construction from 1897 to 1902, Saint Andrews Catholic Church overlooks Roanoke. Among the Gothic-inspired building's fifteen stained glass windows imported from Munich, Germany, are massive ones portraying Saint Andrew and Saint Patrick.

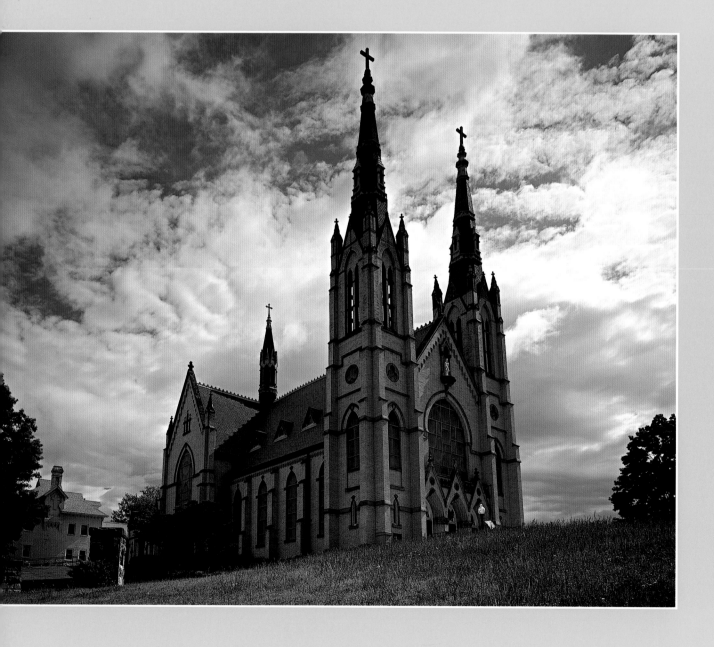

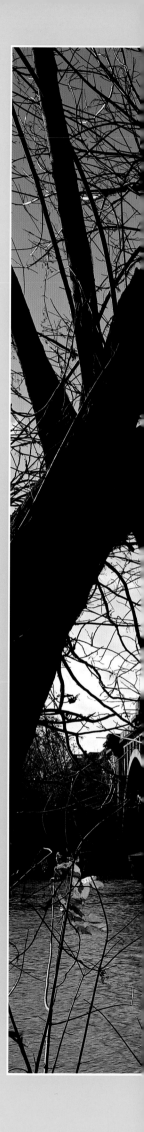

LEFT: In 1861 and 1862, two major Civil War battles at Manassas pitted South against North. The first battle was a Confederate victory when the war was only three months old, and the second was also a Confederate victory thirteen months later. Today the site is preserved as Manassas National Battlefield Park.

BELOW: Near Manassas in Fauquier County, horses enjoy the now-peaceful setting. Virginia's horse population ranks fifth among the fifty states.

ABOVE: Nocturnal and omnivorous, raccoons have adapted well to urban environments, where they raid trash cans. PHOTO BY JUPITERIMAGES CORPORATION

RIGHT: Tupelo trees, which like wet soil and high water, are prized for the delicate honey made from their blossoms. These grow in Great Dismal Swamp National Wildlife Refuge, which extends from southeastern Virginia into North Carolina.

LEFT: Wilburn Ridge rises in Mount Rogers National Recreation Area, which offers trails for horseback riders and hikers, including a stretch of the Appalachian Trail.

BELOW: At the site of the former William J. Carter Farm at Humpback Rocks, the National Park Service recreated a typical mountain farm using historic buildings that were moved and reassembled.

RIGHT: A new day begins in Westmoreland State Park, which extends for one and a half miles along the Potomac River and offers camping, cabin rental, fishing, boating, and interpretive hikes.

BELOW: The three-story Stone House at Manassas National Battlefield Park was a rough-and-ready wagon stop near the busy intersection of the Warrenton Turnpike and the Sudley-Manassas Road. Today it is one of three pre-Civil War buildings standing in the park.

LEFT: In 1607, a contingent of 104 men and boys from England created Jamestown Settlement in the Virginia wilderness. The stories of their hard work and privation and of their Indian neighbors are told today through historical exhibits, reconstructed buildings, and costumed interpreters.

BELOW: Modest in comparison to other Williamsburg buildings, the Tenant House was once a comfortable home for middle-class working people. Interpreters demonstrate their crafts daily inside the building, the only one in historic Williamsburg with absolutely no modern conveniences.

RIGHT: The Satyr Temple sits on the grounds of Chatham Mansion, which became a federal hospital during the December 1862 Battle of Fredericksburg, with Clara Barton and Walt Whitman among the nurses. The home now is in Fredericksburg and Spotsylvania National Military Park.

BELOW: Autumn color blazes in the Blue Ridge Parkway's hardwood forest.

LEFT: Colonial National Historical Park at Yorktown includes Historic Jamestowne and the Revolutionary War's Yorktown Battlefield. Jamestown Memorial Church, seen here, is a 1907 replica of the settlement's 1639 church, which itself had been built on the same site as a wooden church completed in 1617.

BELOW: Eastern redbud and flowering dogwood show off their spring colors. The dogwood was selected as both Virginia's state flower and its state tree.

RIGHT: The Parthenon-inspired Rotunda, designed by Thomas Jefferson, rises three stories above the lawn at the University of Virginia. For many years, the Rotunda housed the university library in its dome.

BELOW: A winter snowstorm contributes to Rappahannock County's forty-some inches of annual precipitation.

LEFT: Virginia produces about a quarter of a billion bushels of corn annually, ranking twenty-fifth among the states.

BELOW: Vines provide green garments for a forest near Jamestown.

FACING PAGE: Looking across the Blue Ridge Mountains from the Appalachian Trail in Jefferson National Forest demonstrates how the mountains earned their name.

BELOW: Fog enwraps Shenandoah National Park.

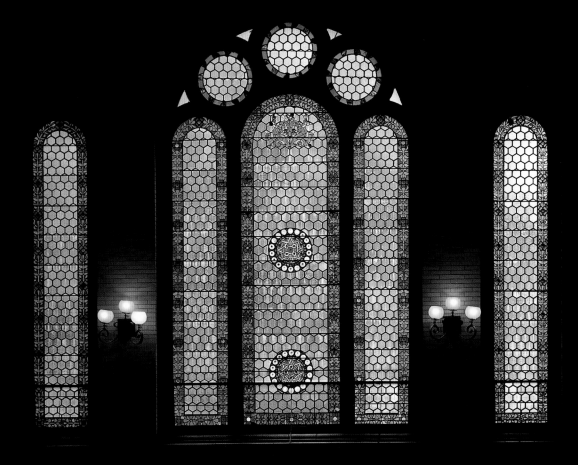

ABOVE: Stained glass glows in Memorial Chapel at Hampton University, which was founded in 1866 as Hampton Normal and Agricultural Institute to educate former slaves. This chapel was built when the school was twenty years old.

LEFT: Farmville, in Prince Edward County, dates from 1798 and today hosts the annual Heart of Virginia Festival of arts, culture, and music on the first Saturday in May.

RIGHT: Centerpiece of the Breaks Interstate Park on the eastern Virginia–Kentucky border is the five-mile-long, 1,600-foot-deep "Grand Canyon of the South," carved 250 million years ago by the Russell Fork River.

BELOW: Constructed in 1931, Memorial House in George Washington Birthplace National Monument stands near the site of the Washington family home. Washington was born on this plantation in 1732 and lived here until the age of three, then returned as a teenaged surveyor-in-training.

ABOVE: Flowstone draperies captivate visitors to Grand Caverns at Grottoes, which have been open to the public since 1806. During the Civil War, General Stonewall Jackson allowed his troops to enjoy the cave system, although he refused to enter.

LEFT: Old Rag Mountain in Shenandoah National Park, one of the Blue Ridge Mountains' highest peaks at 3,291 feet, attracts hikers and climbers to its rocky surface.

FACING PAGE: Crabtree Creek's waterfalls are one attraction of George Washington National Forest.

BELOW: Laurel Creek, in Jefferson National Forest, offers cool comfort for Appalachian Trail hikers.

LEFT: Richmond, capital of the Commonwealth of Virginia, dates from 1607, but also boasts modern business buildings that tower above the James River. PHOTO BY RICHARD NOWITZ

BELOW: Norfolk's MacArthur Memorial includes a museum dedicated to the life, times, and army of General Douglas MacArthur, along with a research library, archives, theater, and classrooms. PHOTO BY RICHARD NOWITZ

RIGHT: At Leesburg, visitors can tour Morven Park's Greek Revival mansion, visit the world's only fox-hunting museum, and marvel at the collection of seventy horse-drawn vehicles from the turn of the twentieth century.

BELOW: The Loudoun County Courthouse, in Leesburg's historic district, dates from 1895. On its grounds are antique stocks and whipping posts—reminders of yesteryear's law-enforcement methods.

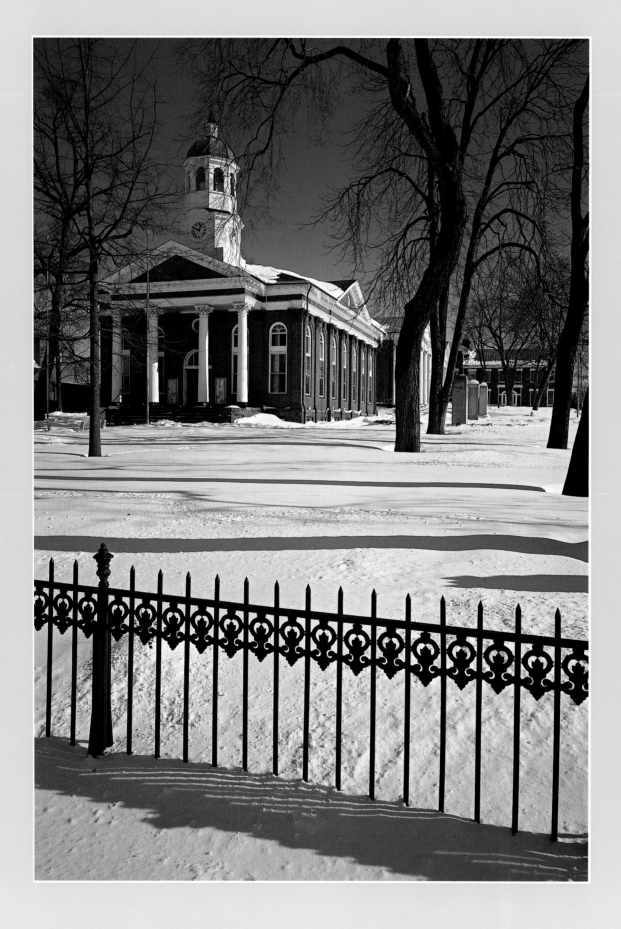

ABOVE: Spring beauty brightens Shenandoah National Park.

LEFT: Rhododendron blossoms frame Crabtree Creek Falls in the George Washington National Forest.

RIGHT: Come and sit for a spell on the porch of the Martha Washington Inn, located in Abingdon. This 1832 home later housed a finishing school, a Civil War hospital, and a women's college before becoming a hotel in 1935.

BELOW: Woodrow Wilson, twenty-eighth president of the United States, was born in this Staunton home in December 1856 and was one year old when his family moved to Georgia.

LEFT: Cows graze on an Appalachian hillside in Giles County.

BELOW: Colonial National Park, which covers most of Jamestown Island in the tidewater region, includes this statue of Matoaka, who was an eleven-year-old girl in 1607 when Englishmen arrived at her home. They called her Pocahontas, which meant "a playful little girl" in the Powhatan language. PHOTO BY RICHARD NOWITZ

RIGHT: This historic log home ornaments tiny New Castle, the seat of Craig County in the Appalachian Mountains.

BELOW: Dog violets flourish along the Maury River in Rockbridge County.

LEFT: At Colonial National Park, visitors explore the replica ship *Susan Constant*, the largest of the three ships that brought Jamestown's first settlers in 1607. The original ship returned to England that same year and continued to serve as a merchant ship for at least another eight years before disappearing from history. PHOTO BY RICHARD NOWITZ

BELOW: Now part of Colonial National Park, Yorktown Battlefield marks the end of British colonization of the future United States, which began nearby at Jamestown. Here, the revolutionary army defeated the British in 1781, winning independence for the thirteen colonies. PHOTO BY RICHARD NOWITZ

RIGHT: A leisurely trail circles Abbott Lake at Peaks of Otter on the Blue Ridge Parkway near Bedford. Rising above the lake are three peaks: Sharp Top (seen here), Flat Top, and Harkening Hill.

BELOW: Many visitors to Shenandoah National Park take the 1.4-mile hike to view Dark Hollow Falls.

RIGHT: Rewards like this overlook await hikers in Shenandoah National Park. PHOTO BY RICHARD NOWITZ

BELOW: Mabry Mill on the Blue Ridge Parkway near Rocky Knob—its sluiceway the study in angles seen here—was opened to run on water power in 1910 by a former blacksmith in the West Virginia coalfields. The self-guided tour along the Mountain Industrial Trail reveals the grist mill, sawmill, whiskey still, and blacksmith shop.

RIGHT: Mount Bleak House was built in 1835 by Isaac Settle as a wedding present for his son Abner. Today it sits in Sky Meadows State Park, near Delaplane, which offers six miles of bridle trails—for those who bring their own horses.

BELOW: The tints and textures of dolomite shale cliffs at Westmoreland State Park, which rise above the Potomac River near Montross.

Hackberry trees, like this one, supplied strong but flexible wood that early settlers used to floor their cabins and to make barrel staves. Hackberries now flourish as shade trees from southern Canada to Florida.

LEFT: Light gilds Gibson Hollow in the Blue Ridge Mountains of Shenandoah National Park.

BELOW: Back Creek reflects autumn colors from the surrounding George Washington National Forest.

RIGHT: With improved management, submerged aquatic plant beds have increased in the Chesapeake Bay's estuaries, where fresh water meets the Alantic's salt water.

BELOW: Most of Virginia's estimated 3,500 to 4,500 black bears live west of the Blue Ridge, with a smaller group roaming near the Dismal Swamp. PHOTO BY ANN AND ROB SIMPSON

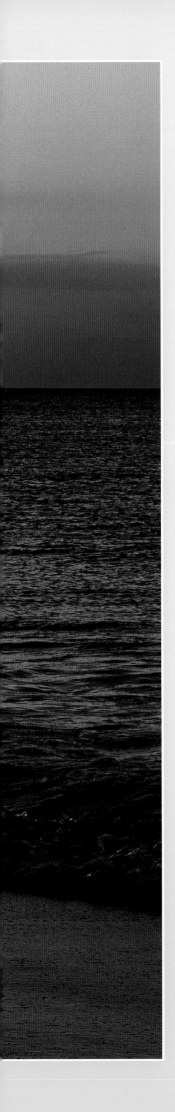

LEFT: A new day begins on thirty-seven-mile-long Assateague Island, an Atlantic Ocean barrier island off Chincoteague, today a designated national seashore. The continuous work of wind and waves has moved the island a quarter of a mile closer to land than it was in 1866.

BELOW: The Shenandoah River rolls placidly under the setting sun.

Completed in 1894, Richmond's Old City Hall includes this seven-story tower. Today the Victorian Gothic structure houses private offices, and visitors are welcome on its first floor.

At the Great Falls of the Potomac River in McLean, the water drops seventy-six feet in less than a mile, the steepest river fall line in the eastern United States.

LEFT: The University of Virginia's neo-Gothic chapel in Charlottesville was dedicated in 1889 and today is used solely for weddings and memorial services.

BELOW: Rockville County sparkles following an ice storm.

ABOVE: Virginia's state bird, the northern cardinal, poses amid dogwood blossoms, the state flower. PHOTO BY ANN AND ROB SIMPSON

RIGHT: A cheery carpet of daisies stretches across a Loudoun County field.

LEFT: Catawba rhododendron blooms along the Blue Ridge Parkway.

BELOW: Four acres of formal gardens in Oatlands Plantation, Leesburg, surround a mansion built in 1804 and remodeled in Greek Revival style in the 1820s.

RIGHT: Designed in the 1920s by the architectural firm of McKim, Mead, and White in keeping with Washington, D.C.'s, neoclassical design, Arlington Memorial Bridge over the Potomac symbolically links the North and the South in its alignment with the Lincoln Memorial and Arlington House, the Robert E. Lee Memorial.

BELOW: Over Albemarle County, threatening beauty rises in a thunderhead illuminated by the setting sun.

RIGHT: When George Washington inherited Mount Vernon, the house stood only one and a half stories tall and held seven rooms. He added a story, including the cupola that "air conditioned" the house when its windows were open, and the two-story piazza for enjoying summer breezes off the Potomac River. It has been restored to its appearance in 1799, the last year of Washington's life.

BELOW: Skyline Drive beckons through the autumn woods of Shenandoah National Park.

RIGHT: St. Luke's Church, in Isle of Wight County, is the nation's only extant example of original Gothic architecture, and the oldest church of English foundation. Known affectionately as the "Old Brick Church," it was built around 1632, and today hosts weddings, concerts, and occasional Episcopalian services.

BELOW: William Byrd II, Richmond's founder, built his James River plantation of Westover around 1730. The Georgian-style house at Charles City is surrounded by tulip poplars now 150 years old.

ABOVE: The Robert E. Lee statue, facing south, was the first memorial dedicated on Richmond's Monument Avenue in 1890. PHOTO BY RICHARD NOWITZ

FACING PAGE: Chesapeake Bay pleasure craft rest in the summer twilight.

RIGHT: Flowerdew Hundred Plantation dates from 1618, when George Yeardley received the original grant and named his land in honor of his wife, Temperance Flowerdew Yeardley. Today the Prince George County site includes an 1850s schoolhouse exhibiting 200,000 artifacts found in three decades of archaeological digs here.

BELOW: Bald cypress, a conifer that annually sheds its scale-like leaves, grows in the swamp at First Landing State Park. Created on Chesapeake Bay by Civilian Conservation Corps workers in the 1930s, this site is where the Jamestown colonists originally came ashore.

ABOVE: A seashell picker's treasure trove spreads along the Chesapeake Bay shore.

LEFT: This rocky shoreline tinted by sunset is part of the extensive Buggs Island Lake, otherwise known as John H. Kerr Dam and Reservoir, that extends from Mecklenburg County into North Carolina.

ABOVE: At Hot Springs in the Allegheny Mountains, The Homestead is both a National Historic Landmark and a luxury resort spa. Development of the seven mineral hot springs began before the American Revolution, and the red brick main building was erected in 1901.

RIGHT: To Thomas Jefferson, Falling Springs in Alleghany County was one of Virginia's most impressive natural wonders. The 205-foot fall is thirty feet taller than Niagara.

LEFT: Georgian-style Chatham Manor, built from 1768 to 1771, is the center of the William Fitzhugh plantation above the Rappahannock River at Fredericksburg. It served as Union headquarters and hospital during the Battle of Fredericksburg and today houses exhibits and offices of Fredericksburg and Spotsylvania National Military Park. Along with Mount Vernon and Berkeley Plantation, it is one of three extant houses visited by both George Washington and Abraham Lincoln.

BELOW: Self-taught architect, president, and all-around scholar Thomas Jefferson was influenced by the Italian Andrea Palladio in designing his hilltop home, Monticello, near Charlottesville.

RIGHT: In the town of Surry, Surry County Courthouse dates from 1923 and is listed on the National Register of Historic Places. The county itself, created in 1652, once extended to North Carolina.

BELOW: The classic Victorian Lee Chapel at Washington and Lee University was commissioned in 1867 by then-president Robert E. Lee. After his death in 1870, he was buried beneath the chapel. His remains later were moved to a family crypt in a building addition.

ABOVE: This trompe l'oeil (French for "deceives the eye") painting portrays a corridor of organ pipes on the front of the compact Tudor organ in St. Luke's Church, Smithfield. The instrument's history dates to 1630, when Sir Nicholas Le Strange purchased it for his manor in Norfolk, England. Annual benefit concerts fund the organ's care and the creation of a replica.

LEFT: A bright field of canola flowers in Hanover County. Canola, or rape-seed, production declined in Virginia during the 1990s but is rising again as the market for healthful canola oil improves.

ABOVE: Dogwood shines through a foggy day in Shenandoah National Park.

RIGHT: In Jefferson National Forest, hemlock and rhododendron trees surround the falls of Little Stony Creek.

LEFT: The Eppes family had fled this home at Appomattox Plantation before it was commandeered by a Union Army quartermaster during the Siege of Petersburg, which lasted from June 1864 to April 1865. Robert E. Lee pulled his troops out of Petersburg on April 2, 1865, and surrendered at Appomattox Courthouse a week later. Today the home is part of Petersburg National Battlefield.

BELOW: Assateague Lighthouse's twin rotating lights shine from the Virginia portion of Assateague Island nineteen miles out to sea and have been functioning since 1833. The building is open to visitors on weekends from Easter to Thanksgiving.

RIGHT: Morning mist rises from a Rappahannock County meadow.

BELOW: Forests, meadows, and wetlands fill Huntley Meadows Park in the Hybla Valley of Fairfax County, attracting wildlife and more than 200 species of birds amid northern Virginia's suburbs.

LEFT: Near Covington in Alleghany County, Humpback Bridge is Virginia's oldest existing covered bridge. Built in 1857, it was part of the James River and Kanawha Turnpike and was the fourth consecutive bridge built at this Dunlap Creek location.

BELOW: Autumn leaves are caught in a Tye River pool near the Blue Ridge Parkway.

RIGHT: The Frontier Culture Museum at Staunton, designed to tell the stories of the commonwealth's major immigrant groups, includes this Irish farm. In buildings dating from the 1700s, living-history interpreters demonstrate the lives of the Scots-Irish people of the Ulster area.

BELOW: Fully grown, these red fox pups will weigh up to fifteen pounds and stand more than two feet tall, doing most of their hunting by night.
PHOTO BY JUPITERIMAGES CORPORATION

LEFT: Roses and irises informally adorn one of Oatland's buildings near Leesburg.

BELOW: White-tailed deer, like these fawns, can be found most everywhere in Virginia.
PHOTO BY JUPITERIMAGES CORPORATION

North Landing River Natural Area Preserve, near Virginia Beach, the Old Dominion's largest such preserve, has been closed because of illegal activity and loss of funding for the Department of Conservation and Recreation.

RIGHT: An autumn mosaic carpets rocks along Shenandoah National Park's Robinson River.

BELOW: Crabtree Falls, between Charlottesville and Lynchburg, drops more than 1,500 feet in several stages—the longest vertical drop in a United States waterfall east of the Mississippi River.

LEFT: Sunlight warms the sandstone Big Schloss ("castle" in German), which sits atop Great North Mountain, 1,500 feet above the Little Stony Creek Valley.

BELOW: The last time this ground was muddy, a raccoon passed this way—along Lake Moomaw in George Washington National Forest.

Fairy Stone State Park offers cabins and tent camping, fishing, boating, and swimming. Its name comes from the naturally occurring x- or cross-shaped staurolite stones—a blend of silica, iron, and aluminum—that past residents treasured as charms for protection against witchcraft.

FOLLOWING PAGES: Once called Woods River, New River is said to have been renamed by Peter Jefferson, father of Thomas, when he was surveying the Virginia–North Carolina border around 1749.

BELOW: Sunrise silhouettes a box elder beside twenty-one-mile-long Claytor Lake in its namesake state park in southwestern Virginia. The lake backs up from a hydroelectric dam built on the New River near Radford in 1939.